D0418796

CHEER UP (IT COULD BE WORSE)

summersdale

CHEER UP (IT COULD BE WORSE)

Copyright © Summersdale Publishers Ltd, 2013

All rights reserved.

No part of this book may be reproduced by any means, nor transmitted, nor translated into a machine language, without the written permission of the publishers.

Condition of Sale

This book is sold subject to the condition that it shall not, by way of trade or otherwise, be lent, re-sold, hired out or otherwise circulated in any form of binding or cover other than that in which it is published and without a similar condition including this condition being imposed on the subsequent publisher.

Summersdale Publishers Ltd
46 West Street
Chichester
West Sussex
PO19 1RP
UK

www.summersdale.com

Printed and bound in China

ISBN: 978-1-84953-375-1

Substantial discounts on bulk quantities of Summersdale books are available to corporations, professional associations and other organisations. For details contact Nicky Douglas by telephone: +44 (0) 1243 756902, fax +44 (0) 1243 786300 or email: nicky@summersdale.com.

TO...*JAMES*...............

FROM...*FRANCESCA*...

xxx

SOME DAYS YOU'RE THE

BUG

SOME DAYS YOU'RE THE
WINDSHIELD

PRICE COBB

TURN THAT FROWN
UPSIDE DOWN
(BY STANDING ON YOUR HEAD)

MOST OF LIFE'S
PROBLEMS
CAN BE *SOLVED*
WITH A NICE CUP OF
TEA & SOME
CAKE

YOU MIGHT NOT THINK SO BUT YOU'RE WONDERFUL

CHIN UP
CHEST OUT
FORWARD HO

THE HARDER YOU
FALL
THE HIGHER YOU
BOUNCE

DOUG HORTON

DON'T SWEAT THE SMALL STUFF

YOU SHOULD ONLY SWEAT AFTER EXERCISE

OR IF IT'S REALLY HOT

IT'S TIME TO PULL YOUR SOCKS UP

RIGHT UP

(TO YOUR **METAPHORICAL KNEES**)

MY GRANDFATHER
ALWAYS SAID THAT LIVING
IS LIKE LICKING HONEY
OFF A THORN

LOUIS ADAMIC

EVEN WHEN YOU
FEEL LIKE A
STALE
BISCUIT

YOU'RE A WONDER MUFFIN

DON'T BLAME IT
ON THE SUNSHINE

KEEP YOUR
AWESOME-TRAIN
ROLLING

YOU'RE
BETTER THAN DIAMONDS
YOU'RE A
MOON
ROCK

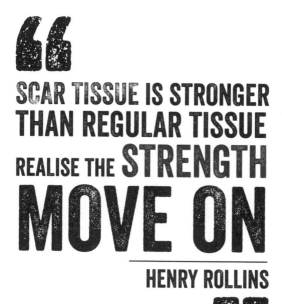

"SCAR TISSUE IS STRONGER THAN REGULAR TISSUE THAN REGULAR TISSUE REALISE THE STRENGTH MOVE ON"

HENRY ROLLINS

IF YOU ARE GOING THROUGH HELL KEEP GOING

WINSTON CHURCHILL

BE
BRAVE!
YOU CAN DO IT

WHEN THINGS GET TOUGH THINK OF PUPPIES!

"SOMETIMES LIFE'S *HELL* BUT HEY! WHATEVER GETS THE MARSHMALLOWS TOASTY

J. ANDREW HELT

"

YOU'RE
50 PER CENT
FAN-DABI-DOZI
AND

50 PER CENT
SPIFFY-TERRIFIC

IF I WERE A WIZARD I'D CONJURE YOU A SMILE

NOW'S THE TIME

FOR DANCING

AND SPLASHING

IN PUDDLES

PEOPLE LIKE YOU
ARE RARE
(LIKE HUMAN UNICORNS)
(HUMICORNS)

ONWARDS

OUTWARDS

UPWARDS

WOULD YOU LIKE SOME CHEERYADE?

TO SUCCEED IN LIFE YOU NEED
THREE THINGS
A WISHBONE
A BACKBONE
AND A *FUNNY* BONE

REBA MCENTIRE

"

IF YOU'RE ALREADY WALKING ON THIN ICE YOU MIGHT AS WELL DANCE

PROVERB

"

KEEP A ROCKIN' AND A ROLLIN'

PERSEVERANCE IS
FAILING
NINETEEN TIMES

AND
SUCCEEDING
THE TWENTIETH

JULIE ANDREWS

IF
PLAN A
DOESN'T WORK
THE ALPHABET HAS
ANOTHER 25 LETTERS

GRUMPINESS LOOMING? LOOMING? *RELEASE* EMERGENCY KITTENS

YOU CAN
DEFINITELY DO IT
I KNOW
BECAUSE I LOOKED
INTO YOUR FUTURE
AND YOU COME OUT
ON TOP

WORSE THINGS
HAVE HAPPENED
AT SEA
(E.G. GIANT OCTOPUS ATTACK)

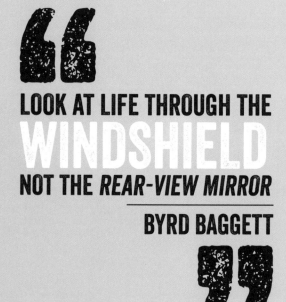

"
LOOK AT LIFE THROUGH THE
WINDSHIELD
NOT THE *REAR-VIEW MIRROR*

BYRD BAGGETT
"

WE'RE HERE FOR A
GOOD TIME
(NOT A *LONG* TIME)

IT'S NOT ALL DOOM AND GLOOM (IT CAN BE FUN AND SUN)

"

WE LIVE IN A
RAINBOW
OF CHAOS

PAUL CÉZANNE

"

SERVING SUGGESTIONS FOR LIFE:

SUNNY SIDE UP

AND WITH TOAST

THE AVERAGE PENCIL IS SEVEN INCHES *LONG*
WITH JUST A HALF-INCH ERASER
– IN CASE YOU THOUGHT OPTIMISM WAS DEAD

ROBERT BRAULT

LET'S
MOVE FROM
SADSVILLE TO
HAPPYTOWN

YOU ROCK
SO DON'T SING THE BLUES

IN THE ORDER OF
AWESOME THINGS
IT GOES
YOU
YOUR SMILE
YOU AGAIN

" WHAT DO WE LIVE FOR
IF IT IS NOT TO MAKE LIFE LESS
DIFFICULT FOR EACH OTHER?

GEORGE ELIOT

LET RIP
WITH YOUR
HAPPINESS

THERE'S NOTHING THAT A **TALL DRINK** (AND A FEW SHORT ONES) **WON'T FIX**

"

DON'T GET YOUR
KNICKERS IN A K_NO_T
NOTHING IS SOLVED
AND IT JUST MAKES
YOU *WALK* FUNNY

KATHRYN CARPENTER

"

"WHEN LIFE LOOKS LIKE IT'S

FALLING

APART

IT MAY JUST BE

FALLING
IN
PLACE

BEVERLY SOLOMON

"

WITH MODERN HEALTH AND SAFETY REGULATIONS THE LIGHT'S NOT ONLY AT THE END OF THE TUNNEL BUT AT REGULARLY SPACED INTERVALS THROUGHOUT

ARE YOU GOING TO LOSE THAT

SAD-FACE

OR SHALL I *TICKLE* IT OUT OF YOU?

**ALL OF US
COULD TAKE A LESSON
FROM THE WEATHER**
IT PAYS **NO ATTENTION** TO CRITICISM

————

ANONYMOUS

YOUR LIFE IS AN OCCASION

RISE TO IT

SUZANNE WEYN

DON'T BE BLUE
BE ALL THE COLOURS OF THE
RAINBOW

IT'S TIME TO LOOK AT LIFE WITH AN *EXPRESSION* OF STEELY RESOLVE

IF LIFE WERE A FILM
THIS WOULD BE THE BIT WITH THE
UPLIFTING
MONTAGE

"
YOU HAVE TO *GO ON*
AND BE CRAZY
CRAZINESS
IS LIKE HEAVEN

JIMI HENDRIX

TIME IS A GREAT HEALER

(AND SO IS ICE-CREAM)

" TO LIVE IS SO STARTLING

IT LEAVES LITTLE TIME FOR ANYTHING ELSE

EMILY DICKINSON

I LIKE IT BEST WHEN YOU'RE HAPPY

I LIKE THE
CUT OF YOUR
JIB

LET'S TURN YOUR DUVET DAY INTO A GROOVY DAY

THE GLASS IS
HALF-FULL

WHAT A
SLAP-UP
WHIZZ-BANG
WORLD THIS IS

IF WE'RE ALL MADE OF
STARDUST
YOU MUST BE MADE OF
SUPERNOVAS

LIFE IS A ROLLERCOASTER

TRY TO EAT A LIGHT LUNCH

DAVID A. SCHMALTZ

YOU CAN'T CHANGE THE PAST

(BECAUSE **TIME TRAVEL**
IS STILL AT THE DRAWING-BOARD STAGE)

YOUR
SUNNY SMILE
SENDS ME

HIGH
SKY

"

THERE ARE DAYS WHEN IT TAKES
ALL YOU'VE GOT
JUST TO *KEEP UP*
WITH THE LOSERS

ROBERT ORBEN

"

I THINK YOU'RE JIM DANDY AND PEACHY KEEN

KEEP ON
KEEPIN' ON

IF YOU'RE INTERESTED IN FINDING OUT MORE ABOUT OUR
GIFT BOOKS, FOLLOW US ON TWITTER:
@SUMMERSDALE

WWW.SUMMERSDALE.COM